RESILIENCE

Cheryl Reibel

Author: Cheryl Reibel
Illustrator: McLean Fletcher

First Printing: 2020

Website: ReadResilience.com
Email: info@ReadResilience.com

I want to thank my mother Lisa Kushner, my father Joseph Reibel and my own beloved daughters, Gabrielle and Samantha Busch.

I am proud of you and know that you will carry the bravery and tenacity of the Jewish people into the next generation.

Foreword

My grandfather, Viktor Frankl, was a cheerful and loving man who enjoyed the little things in life. He was a dedicated medical doctor, curious about people and their stories. Anyone could call him for his advice. He could be grumpy if bothered before he had his big cup of coffee or if I playfully put smiley stickers on his reading glasses — in this case he transformed the ensuing rare outburst of anger into a passionate meaningful lecture about eyeware care. Whenever it fit a situation, he told a silly joke and spoiled my sister and me with trips to the fairground. After all, teaching discipline was not the job of a grandparent. You might have thought: here is a man who probably had not experienced very bad times in his life, at least not more than the next door neighbor. To me he was a grandfather just as I imagined anybody's grandfather to be.

I was nineteen years of age when my sister and I were invited to present an opening message at a conference on logotherapy, the meaning centered approach to mental health that he had developed as a young doctor. He himself was not supposed to fly any more because of a deteriorating heart condition. So my sister and I went in his place, to read a greeting from him and to meet interesting people. It was on the plane to Toronto, excited about the trip, when I first read Man's Search for Meaning —my grandfather's most personal book. In it he wrote about his experiences as prisoner in four Nazi concentration camps. As his grandson I naturally knew the facts, but that day I realized that my grandfather had been to hell and back.

Many questions went through my mind. How could someone who had been regarded as subhuman, then beaten, almost starved to death, and forever separated from people he loved most, become and remain the humorous, life-affirming person I knew? What went through his mind when he realized that he had to let go of what had kept him alive in the camps: the hope to be reunited with his wife, his mother and his brother? How did he not end up a broken, bitter man?

"He who has a why to live can bear almost any how"—he often quoted these words of philosopher Frederic Nietzsche. Coming back to a bombed-out Vienna, with no one waiting there for him, was worse for my grandfather than his time in the camps; there, at least, the main task had been clear: to survive. But now he had lost his "why", his reason to survive. In those days many people who suffered a similar fate were so overwhelmed by the emotional burden that they put an end to their own lives. An understandable choice, which my grandfather considered as well in the immediate time upon his return. Life did not seem to hold much meaning for him anymore. But he decided to keep going, based on pure faith that perhaps there was still some meaningful task waiting for him in the future. And in order to find out, he needed to live.

All of my own problems seemed so insignificant compared to what he had gone through: the failed math test, being bullied at school, the recent breakup. Yet, these experiences were very painful for me. Knowing his story, how could I let these things bring me down? I found out that I was not the only one who asked these questions, when my grandfather told me this story:

In the early 1950s, my grandfather was invited to give a lecture to a group of psychiatrists in the United States for the first time. The host approached him afterwards and asked him a strange question: "Dr. Frankl, have you noticed that the people seemed a little distant, you could even say cold?" "Yes", my grandfather replied. "And aren't you wondering why that is the case?" the host asked. My grandfather assumed the majority of the audience were traditional psychoanalysts, and his methods were quite different from those. But that was not the reason. The host told him: "You, doctor, went through terrible suffering, surviving the concentration camps of Auschwitz and Dachau, losing everything and almost dying. You suffered gravely and you have overcome it. The people in the audience did not. The reason is envy." Startled, grandfather gave this some thought, and then said something he often felt the need to repeat from that day on: "Everyone has their own Auschwitz."

What he meant was that suffering cannot be compared among different individuals. Regardless of how small your own worst adversity may be compared to someone else's, it still is the worst adversity of your life. Sooner or later, every single one of us goes through experiences of suffering that we cannot control. Our suffering may be the loss of things we treasure, or the illness or death of a beloved person. Sometimes we struggle with feelings of guilt, when we make a wrong decision and are forced to face the consequences of our actions. No matter of how we look at it, unavoidable suffering is part of life. And while the cause and experience of your suffering might be unique, different from mine, the overall effects upon us are similar.

My grandfather taught me that there are different ways to respond to the pain of unavoidable suffering. If we can find some meaning in it—for example by looking at a bad experience as a lesson in life, as something we learn from for the future—then the pain we endure is no longer completely meaningless. We transform something meaningless into something which can help us, and others, when adversity and setbacks occurs in the future. There might even come a day we will be glad that a difficult time occurred and turned us in a different, better, direction. Not in spite of, but because of what happened to us. This my grandfather often called the "defiant power of the human spirit".

Eventually, his own tribulations and losses helped him become even better at helping those in despair, those who could not see any meaning in their lives. Today I myself can see how life always provides us with opportunities to find and fulfill meaning, be it by what we put into this world, the works we create, the experiences we share such as love, and the attitudes we choose in difficult times. Life, even in the best of times, asks new questions every day, confronting us with opportunities and challenges, big and small. How we respond is what matters, whether we see ourselves only as the victims of life´s circumstances, or as their co-creators; whether we take good things for granted, or appreciate what we have.

I am often asked how my grandfather passed on his knowledge. He lived it. And I—just as anybody close to him— could learn by simple observation and how he treated others. He completely trusted my ability to make my own choices just as much as he trusted his own. I sometimes wondered about how he could have so much faith in others. After all he went through, who could have blamed him for never trusting any fellow human being ever again?

The answer can be found in the way he looked at human nature. In his view, nobody is completely good or evil. But as human beings we are capable of both, and always free to choose between them. Following the voice of our conscience might not be the easiest path and often leads in a different direction from the majority of people.

This book is set in a time in which the majority of a nation followed the path of Adolf Hitler and his National Socialist Movement. While most of those who had not been declared enemies chose to accept or approve of what was happening, there also were those few who listened to what the voice of their conscience spoke to them and acted accordingly. They were well aware, that for their lonely fight against the injustice and atrocities going on around them, they would have to be willing to pay with their own lives. Most of them did.

One may wonder: Are there injustices and cruelties in today´s world, which the majority of people accept or choose to ignore? Who are the people, the heroes, listening to their conscience instead of trying to just "fit in"?

In 1988, there was an special event commemorating the 50th anniversary of Austria´s annexation into Nazi Germany, at which my grandfather was invited to speak. In his speech he insisted that in every nation, party, race, or group of any kind one can find two kinds of people: decent and indecent. In his view, decent people always were and will probably forever form a minority, and therefore the possibility of another Holocaust always exists. After that speech, a reporter asked him how he, being a psychotherapist, could have such a pessimistic opinion about human nature. He replied that he meant what he said neither in a pessimistic nor an optimistic way, but rather in an "activistic" one: "Isn't it all the more important that each one of us tries his and her best to join this minority of "decent" people?"

This book provides the inspiring story of heroic perseverance in the darkest of times. It is a reminder that even in surroundings of evil and death, at a closer look one can also find hope and love. May we all gain insights from this book and apply them wisely in our own lives. Perhaps then, one day the "minority of decent people" will become a majority after all.

Alexander Vesely
Vienna, September 2020

Introduction

RESILIENCE depicts the stories of Holocaust survivors that I grew up around. My childhood was unique, surrounded by parents, relatives and their friends whose powerful stories of unwavering RESILIENCE and hope in their youth shaped my desire to share these stories. They are their stories of inspiration in such extreme and inhumane circumstances.

These stories of fortitude amidst suffering, kindness amidst cruelty and hope amidst despair were told to me in ordinary places, the people that i knew as my neighbors, friends and family.

I used to hear about them talk about the experiences escaping the ghettos, living of the bounties of the forest and of surviving the dehumanizing hardships of the camps.

I realized that many people are unaware of such narratives. Sharing stories of young Holocaust survivors' strength, I hope will resonate deeply with the reader. RESILIENCE is a set of paintings and short stories that led to the creation of a book to serve as an individual visual tool to broaden a universal education of the Holocaust and show the example of RESILIENCE of these young Jewish people.

The result is a collection of 37 oil paintings and poems depicting each individual story. These 37 represented 2 times 18, translated as Life in Hebrew plus 1 one more to identify a new generation that survived through this horrific time. These poems capture and evoke the innocence and RESILIENCE of these children, surviving even as the Nazis sought to crush both their hope and their lives.

A page in the book next to each story was left open for the reader to have the option to write, illustrate, or create their own personal thoughts.

RESILIENCE, has been taught in public, Jewish, Catholic schools and Universities as well as many teen and adult organizations across the country. The book can be found in Museums, Libraries in the US and abroad as well as the original oil paintings.

It has been more than 70 years since the Holocaust and, one by one, we are losing our survivors to the march of time. This decade may well be the last where we will be able to hear their stories from their own lips. We are losing these wells of strength, wisdom, and humanity, and, already, we are beginning to forget the history of the Holocaust of senseless hate and suffering. But we have a choice: We can all understand and learn from it instead.

The Resilience Project, a 501C3 non profit, seeks to keep the stories of all incredible survivors alive by connecting the past to the present. This work was created in order to increase awareness of the history of hate for no reason and instead to foster unity, open mindedness and individual thinking.

Join me in creating a world of tolerance, kindness, and healing through art. Let's create a world where the tragedy of the Holocaust can, truly, NEVER HAPPEN AGAIN!

Resilience

noun

The ability to recover or adjust easily to misfortune or change.

Table of Contents

The History of the Holocaust   1

The Beginning   2
Beautiful Patch of a Star   3
Ballet   4
Dresses   5
Love at 14   6

The Ghetto   7
My Room   8
My Puppy, Sasha   9
My Daddy's Store   10
Apples   11
Soon the Birds Will Come   12

Escaping the Ghetto   13
In the Snow   14
Shh, Shh   15
Dancing with Leaves   16

Going Into Hiding   17
Sleeping Among Strangers   18
Sweet Stories   19
Our Flowers Will Not Wither   20
We Draw Twigs   21
The Wood Above Us Creaks   22
Church on Sundays   23
Mama, Papa   24
The House is Burning   25

In the Camps   26
The Hidden Ring   27
The Note   28
The Right Line   29
We Will Be Sisters Again   30
Your Heart   31
With My Eyes Closed   32
Every Day a Holiday   33
The Flames are Burning   34

A New Beginning   35
Stripes and Knots   36
Kiss   37
My Soldier and Me   38
Treasures Under the Tree   39
Displaced Person   40
The Orphan Train   41

Hope For The Future   42
Home At Last The   43
Last Stitch Breaks   44
My Little Tree   45

My Father's Story   46
The Righteous Gentile

My Mother's Story   50
The Young Partisan

Acknowledgements   54

The History of the Holocaust

The poems in Resilience take place during World War 2 and the Holocaust (1941-1945 CE) in Germany, Poland, and other areas of Eastern Europe. The children depicted in the poems were also Jewish, an ethnic group that faced constant hardship, discrimination, and violence in that region.

While the poems are meant to be identified with specific people or events, knowing what happened will give you the context for understanding the poems and preventing this terrible history from happening again.

The Beginning

It started by creating differences between people.

ID cards and yellow star badges sewn onto clothes identified Jews for all to see. This allowed the Nazis to isolate Jews as well as other undesirables from the rest of the community.

Once separated, restrictive practices choked the livelihood of affected families and their businesses. Jewish business owners lost their rights to sell to non-Jewish customers – and not long after that, their rights to hold businesses at all.

In the midst of this, young people tried to live and love as best they could.

Beautiful Patch of a Star

3

Mom says it is fun
we will wear the same
dress
everyday
with a beautiful patch of a
star

wow everyone matching

Soon we will all

play games

we are all on the

same
team

Ballet

4

1st position

2nd position

turning

leaping up and down

I am tired

I hate my tights

They itch

My tutu is silly

Ballet tutor is mean

My mother says
continue

It is hard work

Out the window

All my classmates

dancing with their turns

in plain dresses

with stars looking up

they have nice moms

Dresses

5

the big store window
is the same
that used to be us
a mother
and daughter
dancing
She's dressed up
as a bride
falling out of the
dress and shoes

that used to be us

one day we will dance

I will be the
bride
wearing the dress and shoes

that will be us

Love at 14

6

Love at 14
secretly betrothed
to each other
Strings on our wrists
we giggled
we shared dreams
singing dancing food
a beautiful dress and suit
music everywhere

RAID
We scramble
numbers camps
Searching to go home
We all stand
            with no home

Now 18
we have the string still
I see him
          my heart flutters

My betrothed
looks sick

We hold each other
and touch
for the first time

Always my love

We giggled

7

The Ghetto

But eventually Jews had to go.

People were evicted from their homes. Families were forced to leave behind their whole lives and move into crowded, sealed-off communities called "Ghettos."

Children thought that the confinement was temporary. Adults hoped that as long as they worked hard and obeyed the people in authority, they would survive.

They were wrong.

My Room

8

My room
my desk
my chair
my clothes
my books
my secrets
my dreams
my window
my dog
my hopes

my memories to take

I will be back

My Puppy, Sasha

9

Sasha

My puppy

my family

She's just a baby

Too tired
to bark

Her bones
stick out
like mine

I beg to keep her
under my coat

Look I have
room for two

I need to keep her

She is my only
family

My Daddy's Store

10

Stopped at my
daddy's store

all boarded up

I'm happy he stopped
working

Went home to play
with me

Now time for us to play

Went home to find him

the house boarded up

I see him hiding by the side

He calls for me to run
with him

See the people in green

He is Scared

I am not scared

playing with him

Hide and seek

They will never find us

Apples

11

apples
I grew them
I picture it
taste it
so crisp
What colors

So many falling
from the tree

baskets and baskets
Now all I have are
cores
and
pits

I will plant them soon

Soon the Birds Will Come

12

mama and I hike
every Sunday
we always
watch
with delight
for the
birds

thirty times
around the inside
of the ghetto wall

No trees

people in a long line
holding bowls

Maybe for bird seed

Soon the birds will come

Escaping the Ghetto

Eventually forced labor, harsh living conditions, and heartless massacres opened their eyes many realized that they had a terrible choice: Risk death through escaping, or stay…

Escaping the ghetto took many forms: hand-dug secret tunnels, booze-bribed guards, mad rushes to freedom; Men, women, and children tried their chances in hostile, Nazi-occupied lands and freezing snow. Some fled to other countries. Others aligned themselves with resistance movements and fought for their lives.

In the Snow

14

In the dark night
In the snow
my family leaves
one at a time
through the tunnel
we hold the rope
made from socks

off into the woods
Soon the socks
will be mine

Shh, Shh

15

mom and I love the woods
every Sunday we had
walked in the woods
a new game of sh shh
my mother says
everyday we run
from tree to tree
in the woods
        sh shh

That's all we can say
we are moving to the woods
I am so happy
A dream comes true

no more books
no more classes

just running from tree
        to tree
        hiding.

        sh
        shh

Dancing with Leaves

16

I ran so softly

learned in ballet

I am the best

So quiet

I grab the leaves

they are dancing too

we drink the dew

tomorrow I will dance

with the leaves again

Going Into Hiding

Some people chose to hide instead.

Kind people sometimes hid entire families in their houses, in their attics and basements, in old cemeteries, and in shacks. In the thick woods of Belarus whole communities of women and children came to live in bunkers in the forest while their men fought the Nazis as guerrilla troops.

Not all of them made it out and some who hid were found and killed. Children were adopted into non-Jewish families, and even into another religion. This protected them, trading their heritage for their lives.

Sleeping Among Strangers

18

Sleeping among strangers
Cold in a bed
of straw
dreaming of my sister
and puppy

I will leave room for them

Soon they will come to keep me warm

Sweet Stories

19

living
in
a
bunker
in
the
middle
of
the
forest
my
parents
telling
sweet
stories
I
will
remember
these
for
my
children

Our Flowers Will Not Wither

20

Have the seasons changed
the icicles gone
is the warm sun shining
have the flowers begun to bloom
our flowers will not wither

has another year gone by

how old are we
skirts shorter
bodies thinner
behind wood of the kind
under the roof of a killer
our flowers will not wither

Creating colors in the dark
waiting to breathe aloud
only our fingers can move silently
for one more stitch
one more flower
our flowers will not wither

We Draw Twigs

21

Hiding in the woods
we quiet our stomachs

we draw twigs
mine is the shortest

Going for a gold medal

past the smell of the beef stew
head for the trash

pull out the potato peel
and stale bread

make it back to the finish line
in time for dinner

The Wood Above Us Creaks

22

the wood above us creaks
with sounds of large boots
we are beneath the basement
steps

I am the shortest
I go first
my brother holds the gun
my sister holds her breath
I hold steady

soon I will be
tall

to go last

Church on Sundays

23

I walk to
church
on Sundays

I have a new
big home

I have a new
beautiful dress

I have new shiny shoes

I pray on my knees

I eat a wafer

I smile to
my new friends

They say
Pray to Jesus

He too
was once a
Jew

Mama, Papa

24

mama papa
I'm home
it's cold
you are so cold

mama papa
mama papa

I am home

I will wake you again tomorrow

sweet dreams

The House is Burning

25

the house is
burning

my picture is
burning

Flames
cover
my
face

I touch my face

it's hot

my legs too

my skirt curling

there are memories of me

In the Camps

The alternative to hiding was immediate death on cable cars to concentration camps. If someone managed to survive the deadly train ride, they would be killed then and there if they were too weak to work. Family members struggled not to be separated, their bodies were broken by inadequate food, filthy living conditions, and the constant threat of punishment and death.

Thousands of people died every day, and no one knew who would be next…

But they managed to keep their spirits strong.

The Hidden Ring

27

a hidden small ring passed through the cattle car from hand to hand
it comes with a name and a smile
I receive it   Blushing with joy

silence we hear the   rabbi say the prayers   we cannot see each
                                                              other but recite
                                                                    the prayers

woman in the kitchen is wearing my ring
       I check every day
       I know she is saving it for me

                    It is a sign that Jacob is nearby

The Note

28

I hold a pen and paper
wrote a note
We passed

to our children
they read it
We all smile
and cry and hide
tears
Soon it is goodbye
For each one it is a small piece
We smile and vow to put it
together

again

Four
years l er the puzzle
was complete

The Right Line

29

the right line to live
    your age
    30 stay left
    4 stay right

Mother whispers

DO NOT say
  13
  14
SAY

18
19

momma
so
pushy

18

to

the

right

19

to

the

right

to

the

work

camp

We Will Be Sisters Again

30

two girls
strangers in
the camp
no
names

Branded arms
one number apart

not a word between

opposite sides of the

morning line

the line to eat

so little

Passing their rations

between the

weakest

Do Not show
our numbers

we want to stay

we want to keep

our secret

They will not
separate us

we will always be

one number apart

we know soon we will
be sisters again

Your Heart

31

I feel

your heart

Mother is that you

Do you feel mine

Do you see me

too tired
to lift
my hand

too scared to give a
strong glance

Would you know
it's me

Feel
me
please

I see a glance

I feel her heart

With My Eyes Closed

32

With my eyes closed   the dirty water   old bread
Each small bite is my Mother's brisket   potatoes
later they will give no more
Tomorrow I will taste the strudel   Her sweets
Always see her smile   as I taste her food
with my eyes closed

Every Day a Holiday

33

grassy water   stale bread

Shabbat   Rosh Hashanah
          Yom Kippur
                    Sukkot
          Simchas torah

                         Purim
          Passover
                    Hanukkah

     I smile as I eat
          every day a holiday

The Flames are Burning

34

it must be Shabbot
the flames are burning
the smoke fills the sky
so many women
lighting so many candles
they are not leaving
my mother hides with me

says I am too young to go

she is happy not to light them

I don't want her to leave

A New Beginning

But even in these hellish places, people did not completely despair. They kept surviving, kept track of time, looked to the future and survived.

Finally, in the Spring of 1945, the war ended and the survivors – people who had survived years of imprisonment and torture – were finally rescued. Some were able to reunite with their kin and rebuild their lives, but many survivors could not return to their old homes or find their families.

Hundreds of thousands of Jewish orphans were transported into refugee camps in Allied countries and had to start their lives over from scratch. Others were also placed in displaced persons camps. Some fortunate children were adopted by kind people who brought these hurt, battered, distraught young people into their own homes.

Stripes and Knots

36

February 1940

I know the month
I know the year
I count my stripes and
     move the knots

I hear the gate
I see the gray uniforms
I see the yellow stripe
          on the side sleeve

I open my knots

April 1945

Kiss

37

catch a glimpse

we throw a kiss

with blood chapped lips

it is fine

we will kiss soon

when we are home

My Soldier and Me

38

He found me

he freed me

he fed me

he washed and
Clothed me

he loved me

he married me

My soldier
and me

Treasures Under the Tree

39

my family
treasures
candlesticks
pictures
papers
prayer books

buried deep
under
the
tree

I eat the fruit
while they
dig
for our memories
the fruit is my

treasure

and the tree will

always

grow more
for
me

Displaced Person

40

The Orphan Train

41

Hope For The Future

Their new life had its hardships, but the young people who had survived the Holocaust managed to thrive in the future they had waited for.

They had children and grandchildren and, whenever they could they and their children spoke out against atrocity and tried to change the world for the better.

I was one of those children.

I hope that this collection of poems inspired you, too, to join me in preventing this cycle of violence from happening ever again.

Home At Last

43

HOME
at last
just to see
through
the locked gate
through
closed doors
ask to go inside
touch the walls
windows are closed

I SMILE
No locked gate

no closed doors

no walls

NO closed windows

ALL
is open
to go

anywhere

The Last Stitch Breaks

44

the war breaks
the last stitch breaks
their hands break
their hearts break
Promise to never let go breaks

One loves a man
with U.S. papers

The other insists on
Israel

8000 miles
2 continents
2 languages
26 years pass

Grandchildren blossom

A sweet bouquet in the arms
of the righteous

Their flowers did not wither

My Little Tree

45

My little tree
my own little tree
the tree grew for me
in the forest
my initials on it
the small branches
formed a smile
the dew of the leaves
replenished me
I hid behind it
counting the leaves

Fifty years later
I found it
the bark stronger
the smile wider
with too many leaves to count
my initials taller
the dew sweeter

My Father's Story
The Righteous Gentile

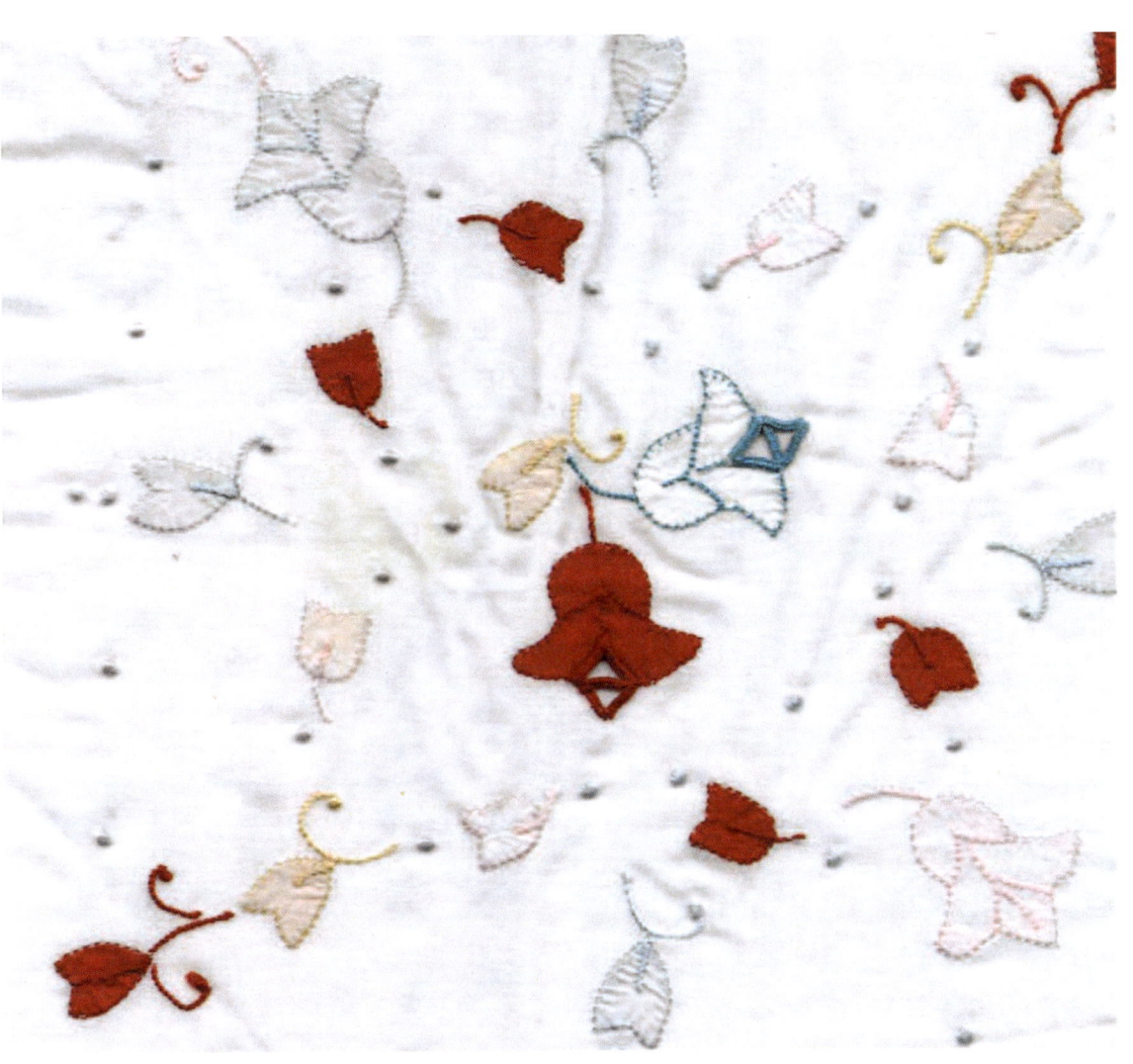

46

Mincha and Pearl Reibel hid in a small dark attic through the Holocaust and World War II – Four years of silence and fear. Janina Rybak, the woman of the house as a close neighbor in the Ukraine, risked her life to hide the two sisters. There was not much she could spare besides food scraps, but at least the girls – and their brothers hiding in a nearby cemetery – would survive and would take turns running for scraps that Mrs. Rybak would purposely leave in the garbage.

Mrs. Rybak was careful not to let her husband, a Nazi Officer, detect anything. She sent away her own child away to a boarding school not to reveal her hiding the girls. When her husband went to work, she would knock on the attic to let them know that they could move about without being heard. To help these young girls keep their hands and minds busy, Mrs. Rybak gave them old linens to embroider. Huddled together, they covered handkerchiefs with beautiful flowers and waited out the war. (Page 20 and 44).

They survived, and the handkerchief they made while in hiding is a testament to the beauty of RESILIENCE.

Janina Rybak is honored by Yad Vashem, a museum complex in Israel dedicated to preserving the memory of the Holocaust. The museum includes the Garden of Righteous which was built to honor those who during the Holocaust risked their lives to save Jews from extermination by the Nazis. In the garden over 30,000 from 51 countries are honored in the garden. The two young women she sheltered were my aunts. The hidden brothers were in a cemetery nearby and risk their lives to get scraps of food that Mrs. Ryback would purposefully leave in the garbage. (Page 21).

When the war ended the four siblings were together and they returned to find their families artifacts that were buried in the woods near their home. (Page 39). They looked into their house and asked to see it. (Page 45). It was occupied by a family who allowed them to go inside. Later, they were sponsored by family members who worked hard to finally locate them in the area where they had lived. They did not want to separate but one sister met and married a man who was determined to go to Israel and become part of Zionist movement. The other sister married a man who was sponsored by a family member to move to Denver and began practicing as a chaplain. The brothers remained together sponsored by cousins in New Jersey.

Years later after the brothers worked very hard they saved up money to bring Mrs. Rybak to America to live with our family for a year. My father brought all the siblings and their families to our house and reunited to spend time with Mrs. Rybak. My father's plan was to take her all around America.

Her only request was that the family members stayed as long as they could with us so she could cook fresh food for everyone everyday because they ate her scraps for four years and now she wanted to feed them as kings and queens. She had no desire to do anything for the year but to shop for food, stay with my family, and cook for us everyday. It was so beautiful that she became the most important person in our family.

My Mother's Story

The Young Partisan

50

My mother, Lisa Kushner, was 11 when the Nazis came. She survived, along with her father, Naum Kushner, and sister, Rae Kushner. My mother worked in the Novogrudok ghetto office and overheard that the next week they were going to shoot all the 216 Jews that were not slaughtered already.

The Jews began building a tunnel in the floor of the barracks while putting the mud in their socks and hiding it to be dispersed at night. (Page 14, 15, and 16). Through the tunnel they insisted that the younger people go first but my mother and aunt went to the back to make sure my grandfather would get out because he was very weak.

Later, she hid with her family in the thick woods of Belarus and was found by the 4 Bielski brothers, who were brave Partisans combing the woods. They took in everyone of all ages and no matter how sick they were. They built a community of 1200 Partisans over the 1.5 years.

There are now 45,000 descendants and the brothers are honored all over the world for the most remarkable feat that they did.

The story was depicted of the brothers and their Partisan movement in the 2008 movie Defiance, starring Daniel Craig and Liev Schreiber. A Partisan is a freedom fighter who hid and protected Jews during the Holocaust.

After the war, my mother, aunt and grandfather spent four years in a displaced persons camp in Cremona, Italy. There they waited for papers sponsored by HIAS. HIAS is a group that helped these Jewish refugees and advocates for their fundamental rights so they can rebuild their lives.

They filled out papers for them so they may move to America and other countries.

Here they lived with many other adults and children in a one room apartment in Brooklyn. She began working at a fur store in New York as a seamstress, a trade she learned as she repaired Partisan uniforms in the woods. While working she completed a high school degree and sang in the Yiddish theater.

She met my father in a community of survivors and they both saved up their money for four years to get married and rent an apartment together in the basement in Brooklyn. They had two girls there.

Eventually they moved to Elizabeth, New Jersey, an area of other survivors and an opportunity for them. My father always spent the day working with his brother. My parents shared our home with family and lone survivors.

She had an opportunity many years later to return to her hometown with part of her family. (Page 45). My mother went to look for graves of her family and any neighbors that could give her information.

She always felt the importance of sharing her story of her life being only twelve when her family was placed in the ghetto and the good fortune of being found by the Bielski brothers and after years had her sponsorship to start a hard life in America.

She shared her stories of RESILIENCE with schools of all religions and ages also sponsored by politicians to travel to tell her story. She made a tape for the Shoah Foundation library, found on Google as well. She returned to Poland with the help of the Partisan Educational Fund to possibly find the family graves and any information leading to the ghetto. She would teach, "Never again" with all of her conviction, "let us never forget." Her teaching was to avoid the mistake of following the past and to unite people to learn that hatred should not exist.

She has since passed, but her words still resonate through my mind and hopefully all that she shared her story with.

By using the combined mediums of poetry and illustration, Resilience was written to speak to the heart.

These stories of fortitude amidst suffering, kindness amidst cruelty and hope amidst despair should be remembered.

My mother's words, "Never again and let us never forget" should resonate through your mind as well. We must find the commonalities that bind us together, the basic humanity that connects us all across distance and time.

I hope these poems inspire you to reach a better future together and never forget.

Acknowledgements

I would like to pay my respect to the 6 million Jews who lost their lives to Hitler's brutality. All survivors, all children of survivors, and the righteous souls who risked their lives to protect the persecution of the Jewish people. The Partisan brigades as the Bielski brothers should also be honored for their selfless strength to save over a thousand people who were hiding in the woods. Those who fought injustice should never be forgotten. We should all have my deepest admiration and gratitude for their bravery and RESILIENCE in the face of hardship.

I want to personally thank the incredible survivor families of my youth of Elizabeth and Hillside New Jersey whose mission has been to preserve the history of the Jewish people and all the people who risked their lives and this terrible genocide by building museums, houses of worship, organizations and schools around the world.

Acknowledgements

Ultimately, this project would not be possible without the hard work of a very talented young artist, McLean Fletcher, a world recognized contemporary artist, whose beautiful oil paintings brought these stories to life.

Thank you all so much.

I hope that these stories and illustrations foster unity and hope for the future allowing for this to NEVER HAPPEN AGAIN!

About the Author

Growing up in a community of Holocaust survivors, Cheryl was immersed in their tales of courage and survival. By tapping into these childhood memories and bringing these stories to life as poems, Cheryl seeks to empower the next generation to build a better, kinder world.

As her two daughters move into their adult lives, she can already see glimmers of change for the better.

About the Artist

The artist McLean's simple yet bold style helps bring out the compassion, innocence and inner strength shown in RESILIENCE. McLean is featured in galleries worldwide and written up in an international publication as an emerging contemporary artist.

She hopes to change the world through her art by interpreting these stories of young survivors.

www.ingramcontent.com/pod-product-compliance
Lightning Source LLC
LaVergne TN
LVRC101630141224
799067LV00030B/142